Thriving in C[illegible]racy

Overc[illegible]n the Placement[illegible]Curates

Jon J Marlow

Director of Ordinands and Vocations Officer
for the Diocese of Canterbury

GROVE BOOKS LIMITED
RIDLEY HALL RD CAMBRIDGE CB3 9HU

Contents

Dedication
For Rod, who unconditionally shared his ministry with me,
and Wendy, who gave me the gift of seeing my ministry through fresh eyes.

First Impression October 2020
ISSN 2041-0972
ISBN 978 1 78827 141 7

1

Thriving in Curacy?

> I have had an excellent experience in my curacy and am very grateful for my time. My incumbent has been a wise guide and very encouraging.

A good curacy, such as that described above, is a joy to behold! Both the new minister and their training incumbent (TI) come out of it excited and re-energized for their future ministries. Such a curacy involves the curate being able to use their gifts, while learning new skills and fully sharing in the pastoral, liturgical and teaching ministry of the TI. At the same time, they are encouraged to develop and lead in an area of their own. They are present at the table as strategic decisions are made, learning how to share leadership with colleagues and volunteers.[1]

While it can be tempting for a TI to want curates who resemble themselves, there can be healthy creativity when TI and curate complement each other. Of course, this requires a TI to know how to facilitate and release someone with different gifts from them, rather than to clash or feel threatened. At their best, training incumbencies finish not only with a profound sense of job well done but also of healthy, joyful grieving at the loss of the training relationship.

However, not all curacies go as planned, and not all curates leave their placement revved up for their future ministry. For my Doctor of Theology and Ministry course at Durham University, I conducted a small-scale research project in 2017. Through an online survey and follow-up interviews I explored issues surrounding the placement of curates and how problems in curacies may be anticipated, overcome or avoided.[2]

What I Discovered

Central to the survey were three questions. Curates were asked whether they agreed or disagreed with the following statements:

- I would recommend my TI to train other curates.
- I would describe the relationship with my TI as positive.
- I have been happy in my curacy overall.

Of the 56 respondents, an encouraging 65% said they would recommend the TI, 70% described their relationship as positive and 67% felt their curacy had been happy overall. However nearly a third (35%, 30% and 33%, respectively) could not agree with the statements, a higher percentage than recent research had predicted.[3]

Having worked alongside curates and ordinands in a variety of roles, I wanted to explore the underlying causes of these challenges. Ultimately, the survey and interviews revealed five potential difficulties which, if recognized early enough, can go some way to preventing or alleviating common problems.

2 Five Potential Difficulties

Here, then, are the five predictable potential difficulties revealed by the survey.

TIs might not recognize that curacies are a process of adult education, and that learners are highly trained and motivated to learn

This has several different manifestations, some explicitly articulated and others more subconscious. TIs can assume a training model which is best characterized as master/apprentice or even parent/child. This model does not recognize that the curate comes with a wealth of skills and experiences of their own, and may even be better equipped to minister in a collaborative way than their TI. Johnny reflected on the differences between his college training and his curacy, saying:

> I would suggest that my [initial] training was geared towards a more collaborative model. Thus, one of the potential struggles derived from the need to adjust my expectations after college.[4]

Beverley found that diocesan expectations about models of ministry were not shared at a local level:

> Our bishop was saying...that there needed to be a joined-up process in placing us, both as curates and beyond and that we were not apprentices, we were preparing for an unknown future and a different way of doing ministry...The training was...for a different style of ministry, for collaborative ministry, and trying to get us to look at what our strengths were. The bishop was saying that, and then I didn't find it on the ground—twice!

Curates also reported the ways their TIs' words had reinforced the old model. Beverley recalled her TI saying, 'I say these things because they are the things that worked for me, so what you need to be is be an apprentice who watches what I do.' Philip was told at the outset of his curacy that, 'You'll probably find there will be quite a lot of deskilling' as his TI perceived the unlearning of previous skills to be a necessary part of the training process. Lesley identified this as wider than simply a local problem, saying:

> At no point in any of my two selection processes...did I feel that anything I had done before was of any value or affirmed by the church. So, I went in pretty undervalued.

Some TIs do not take a collaborative approach to ministry

Curates tend to leave initial training with the expectation that ordained ministry will be a meaningful collaboration between stipendiary and self-supporting clergy and teams of lay people. What they often encounter in their curacy is a TI who is operating as a sole practitioner, even within a team ministry or multi-parish benefice. This can simply be because the incumbent has never known anything different themselves.

Sometimes miscommunication occurs when the same words were being used to mean different things by different people. Following a critical comment she had written in her end of year report, Beverley was asked by her TI what she meant by collaborative ministry:

> And I said, 'Well, you sit down and you talk through things and you make a collaborative decision.' He said, 'I haven't got time for that.' No, that's my point. It does take time, but it also saves time, because you don't all do everything.

Another area in which curates may not be treated as colleagues is when their church tradition or spirituality is not respected as equally valid to that of their TI. In their responses to the survey, one curate complained that their spirituality was 'unsupported' and 'rubbished' by their TI. Another said:

> Central to my faith and churchmanship is the eucharist, which [my TI] has consistently played down. She does not like the daily office or any other commitment to sharing daily prayer and so my efforts at this have been constantly thwarted.

Hannah remembered her TI saying, in front of parishioners, 'I have never set foot in an evangelical church and never would, because I hate evangelicals.' She went on to elaborate that if she had known this at interview she would not have taken the curacy.

Some clergy are made TIs despite evident relational difficulties

Clergy are chosen to be TIs for a variety of reasons, some unrelated to their suitability to be a trainer. Some clergy feel they need a curate to share the workload. Others may perceive it as recognition of seniority or that they are working in an established training parish. This can place diocesan officers in a difficult position, experiencing pressure to place a curate with the TI, even if they are not a good match.

Sometimes, tensions within parishes and ministry teams are known locally but not reported to diocesan officers. As Martyn Percy comments, tensions can be overlooked due to a mixture of 'denial and collusion, with a bit of inertia thrown in.'[5] Several curates in the study reported problems that were already well-known and which, with hindsight, they saw that diocesan officers were alluding to in conversations before the curacy. Veronica reported that her TI announced he was leaving for a diocesan role within a week of her ordination; Beverley was told by her archdeacon that, 'It's problematic you coming here,' despite feeling pressured into the role. Martin was placed with a TI who was known to be suffering from stress.

Diocesan officers and materials can perpetuate the myth that problems are rare and are merely part of the sacrifice of ministry

Beverley comments that she had 'spent a lot of time thinking I was the only one having a hard time' and that this was reinforced by the 'rhetoric that was coming from the diocese and nationally about doing things differently.' Despite the received understanding that it is common for curacies to experience problems, statements like this one still appear in diocesan briefings for curates:

> In 99% of cases where curacies founder (and fortunately there are not that many) they do so because of personal, relational issues.

However well-meaning they are, such statements deny the experience of a third of the curates in this study. Those who had the opportunity to compare notes with others could even perceive this as the church deliberately turning a blind eye. Those with less developed support networks can find their problems compounded by the belief that they really are the only one who is struggling in this way.

A lack of support due to confused lines of accountability

Issues which are addressed when they first occur can more easily be prevented from becoming problems that need intervention from diocesan officers and senior staff. The practice of appointing a facilitator or work consultant to meet with both the curate and TI is a welcome step from many dioceses. However, it requires a combination of self-awareness and lack of defensiveness on the part of the TI to work well. Lesley's experience was that, even when she prepared for the mediated supervision, the consultant was not able to facilitate honest discussion:

> We had supervised supervisions and...I said to [the spiritual director] afterwards, 'Why did you not say anything? I gave you ample opportunity to ask the questions that would have opened up the discussion about what was going on between us, but you never, you never did that.' And she said, 'Yeah, I recognized something was going on but I didn't step in.' And it took me a year to come to terms with the fact that I was scared of my own training incumbent.

Facilitated peer-reflection groups can also help, although the perception is that, beyond the catharsis of talking about the problem, very little actually changes as a result of airing problems in this setting. Similarly, curates are frequently asked how they are doing in a variety of contexts, but seldom in an environment or manner that welcomes an honest answer from those experiencing difficulties. Veronica reported an informal conversation in which she had told her archdeacon that her curacy was 'not going particularly well.' The next time they met, the archdeacon said, 'I won't ask how you are, in case you tell me.' Beverley recalled that her IME officer had delayed for four months before responding to a request for help in her first curacy, which eventually broke down. She said, 'He sat us down together and tried to do a go-between thing. The ship had sailed by that point, he left it too long.'

Clearly these are not universal experiences, but a third of curates describing these issues makes it vitally important to understand the problems and provide suggestions for how to address them. The following chapters will endeavour to do so by offering practical strategies whereby those involved in the placement and training of curates can avoid these five mistakes. Having addressed ordinands seeking a placement, training incumbents, diocesan officers and curates themselves, I then draw some resources for clear communication into a relational toolkit for curates and TIs to work through together.

Advice for Ordinands, Incumbents and Dioceses

3

Ordinands: Look Before you Leap

The question of where you will serve your curacy often begins to surface in the final term of your penultimate year at theological college. For those on a two-year course this can seem disconcertingly soon after you started training. Fortunately, the days when ordinands were summoned to the principal's office to be assigned a placement are behind us, but the process still carries an air of mystery, compounded by the inevitable comparison with colleagues and anxiety about being left behind or shoehorned into an ill-fitting curacy.

Feeling pressured to accept a specific curacy was a common experience among those who were experiencing problems with their TI. They reported feeling rushed into making a decision about the curacy on offer or even being told it was this job or nothing. For some there was no suggestion that they could take time to consider the role or talk with others about whether the training relationship seemed like a good fit for them and their ministry.

Hannah, despite recognizing the support that her Theological Education Institution (TEI) had given her in the process, said, 'I wish somebody would have compiled a list of questions for us to ask our incumbent or told us that we didn't have to take that job.'

When meeting a potential TI for the first time, it will be tempting to ask questions about the practicalities of the role, but generally these things can be sorted out later and recorded in a working agreement. Instead, my suggestion is to use the formal interview time to ask questions which will help you make an informed decision about whether this TI and placement are a good fit for you. Given that ordinands will typically meet a potential TI over a single day or a weekend, the following questions are designed to open up a discussion about your potential TI's model of training and approach to collaboration:

- What metaphor would you use to describe the curate–TI training relationship?
- What is unique about the curate–TI training relationship?
- What would your ideal ministry team look like?
- What do you think I will be able to learn from you?
- What types of people do you find it hard to work with?

At the interview, please take seriously the advice which you should have heard again and again during your journey to this point—'This is a two-way process of discernment.' It may feel that the power dynamics are such that you are unable to ask the questions you really want answered, but begin modelling in the interview what you hope to find in your curacy. If you are confident to try a direct approach then, fairly near the start of the conversation, I would say something like, 'I've got five questions that I'd really like to know the answers to by the end of our time together today.' If you prefer a more low-key approach, then maybe end your answers to a few of their questions with questions of your own. If you are not able to ask your questions or find they are not welcome or taken seriously, then listen carefully to what that tells you. Take Maya Angelou's oft-repeated advice, 'When someone shows you who they are, believe them the first time.'

Above all, give yourself space to make this important decision and take time to reflect and pray with friends, family and colleagues from your TEI. Again, it can be difficult to balance respecting confidentiality with gathering support for your decision. What I would suggest is gathering a group of supporters who know you well before you begin the process of looking for a curacy. Having stressed the importance of confidentiality to them, you can then come to them throughout the process for prayer, advice and encouragement without having to do the awkward dance where you try to avoid admitting there is anything to tell.

Having taken the time you need to make a prayerful decision, do not be afraid to say 'no' to a placement, even if this prolongs the period of waiting and uncertainty as you look for the right place. You may need to be prepared to justify this decision to your bishop or diocesan director of ordinands (DDO), so dig below the feeling of unease and try and put your finger on exactly what the warning signs were for you. This will be helpful for them, especially if they have other curates who might be offered that same placement.

Once you have accepted a placement you can relax a little, although the temptation in liminal situations is to move into the new role emotionally at the expense of finishing well where you are. As this period can last many months, this is worth paying attention to.

Training Incumbents: Ministry Under a Magnifying Glass

Recent research found that TIs tend to find training a curate a more rewarding experience than their curate does.[6] This suggests that TIs are less likely to realize that problems are entering into the training relationship. As discussed in chapter two, the root of these problems can sometimes be the model of training that the TI is operating or their inexperience working with teams in a collaborative way.

When I was at theological college, an ordained friend told me, 'All you need to do to be loved as a curate is to be good at one thing which your vicar isn't.' A curate who was training with me was passionate about pastoral visiting, which balanced my own inclination to focus my attention on other areas of ministry. In such a situation the result can be a stronger team and a positive learning experience for you and your curate.

A central element in the formation of your curate is the opportunity for them to have no-holds-barred access to you and to observe your ministry from close quarters. This has the effect of holding up a magnifying glass which can often reveal flaws that were previously invisible to the naked eye. This can be intensified if your curate has strong skills in an area where you are weaker. In order for this scrutiny to lead to a positive outcome there is a need to be 'undefended' in your leadership, to welcome those whose presence offers a critique to [your] own ministry, and to see that having a curate is an opportunity for mutual learning.[7]

If this does not happen, it is possible for the training to become a power play, reinforcing the hierarchical nature of the relationship. Lesley reported that her TI called her 'Curate' or addressed her, 'By my title, which ranked lower than hers.' She reflected that, 'You could say, "Oh, that's just being oversensitive," but the way in which it was used very much kept the pecking order.' Philip had a similar experience:

> I have lost count of the number of times when she said, in front of other people, to me, 'Don't forget I write your reference'...or if ever I did something, she would say, 'I taught you well.'

As a TI, you need to recognize the training and expertise of your curate, find ways to use and develop their skills and be open to learning yourself through the relationship. A helpful dialogue partner here is the world of adult education, which introduces a number of assumptions which are relevant to training curates. These are:

- that adult learners take responsibility for their own lives and their own learning;
- have relevant previous experience, and;
- are motivated to learn where they see the real-world application of theory.[8]

TIs who are effective trainers will naturally espouse this approach to the training of curates, or will warm to it when they see it modelled or hear it explained.

Biblical models of leadership also offer a critique to the infantilizing parent/child model of training and the hierarchical ecclesiology which underpins it. In a survey of biblical models of supervision, Alan Wilson calls TIs to paradigms such as teacher, steward and mediator which empower and free the curate.[9] Leadership can be directive but passes on responsibility. The image of the shepherd is a particular reminder that curates sometimes need guidance and directive. The relationship is not one of complete equality, although collaboration should be a more obvious feature than direction.

Ajith Fernando couches collaborative ministry in terms of receiving help, of being vulnerable and sharing weaknesses rather than perpetuating an unequal hierarchy.[10] Louise observed how her conscious collaborative practice had helped her TI adapt his own model of ministry, at least for the time being:

> In the first year as a deacon I got to do things like take Morning Prayer and other things that I could do that you didn't have to be priested for... so, as soon as I was priested, I got lay people to do those jobs. And for a lot of them it was the first time that they had been asked to do that. And, I think, probably, that's changed [my incumbent] as well because he's now got lots of lay people doing things.

TIs for whom operating collaboratively is a new experience may be helped to refine their own model of ministry by the presence of someone who has been more recently trained and has professional experience from outside the church. As a self-supporting curate, Lesley found that it took a long time before she was accepted as someone who could provide leadership at that level:

> What strikes me is that I had everything they ever needed...but it was the recognition that I had what they needed, and their recognition that they needed me. I always thought that what I knew in terms of teams was highly missional. Here was a culture that required transformation, and I had the knowledge to enable that, which, four years on, is starting to happen.

The watchword for TIs approaching a new curate relationship is self-reflection. Take time to examine how you are reacting to your curate:

- Are you feeling the need to rein them in?
- Are they asking for things which you feel are unreasonable, or which you do not have time for?

- Do you feel a sense of frustration or even anger or inadequacy around them?

If you can answer 'yes' to any of these questions then please do not assume that this is just your curate's problem. Instead, take the opportunity to see what is going on in your own heart and talk it over with a spiritual director or other impartial colleague. Modelling self-reflection, vulnerability and seeking spiritual support are important parts of your curate's training.

As the person chiefly responsible for their formation and training at this stage of their ordained ministry, your job is to release them into their calling, not shoehorn them into yours.

Questions for Reflection

Whether you are a seasoned training incumbent or newer to the role, the following exercise is designed to help you reflect on your current training relationship, explore your own motivations and recognize what is going on below the surface. You can use it alone, in the manner of an *examen* prayer, or answer the questions with a trusted support group, mentor or spiritual director. Each training relationship will be different, so think about your current curate as you work through the questions.

- Think of one thing your curate is better at than you are. What is it?
- When do you start to feel irritated by your curate? (What does that reveal about you?)
- What are you reluctant to let them do? (What do you think will happen?)
- What can you learn from your curate at the moment?
- What does your curate need from you right now? (If you cannot answer that then you need to ask them.)
- Lastly, do remember to pray for them, daily.

A Prayer for Your Curate

O God who calls
All people to come to him
I thank you for *[N]*
For his/her/their calling to be
A shepherd of your flock,
Serving as your co-worker
And ambassador.

I thank you for the gifts
You have given *[N]*
Especially I thank you for their gifts of..............................
I pray that you would grow
in them the gifts of............................
That they may serve you more faithfully
in the church and the world.
I pray for their character,
That they may grow in love for you
And for your people
And for those who do not know
Your loving kindness and mercy.
I thank you for the ways they show me
How I need to grow and change
And I pray for their future ministry.
I thank you for the passion
You have given them for ....
And I ask that they would continue
To reflect the likeness of your Son
And recognize his image in the faces
Of those they will go on to serve.
Please bless our partnership
As we travel this road together.
Help me to give of myself selflessly
And to pray that I may see you
Working powerfully through *[N]*
Now and in the future. Amen.

Dioceses: Matchmaking and Picking Up the Pieces

Fairly or unfairly, much of the blame for unhappy curacies seems to be directed at those who arrange and oversee placement, especially senior staff and diocesan officers. While problems can occur in placements without the Bishop, DDO or IME Director ever being aware of them, many of these can be anticipated by keeping in mind the five common difficulties in arranging curacies. It is the responsibility of diocesan senior staff and officers to anticipate and overcome these.[11]

A good training incumbent is an invaluable asset to any diocese. On the flipside, clergy who have not developed effective models of collaborative working and lay teams in their own ministry are unlikely suddenly to develop the skills to treat a curate as an ordained colleague. A good indicator of this can be the reasons TIs give for wanting a curate. For example, Beverley's TI expressed it by saying, 'How am I expected to do, to be able to do this on my own?' and 'I can't do this on my own.' This could be revealing either a situation in which they have become overloaded or an inability to share ministry tasks. There is no guarantee that simply introducing a curate will alleviate rather than exacerbate either circumstance.

Creating a Supportive Environment

While the survey sample was small, a high level of dissatisfaction was found in all four participating dioceses, suggesting a pattern which is likely to be indicative of problems across the wider Church of England. Thus, all TEIs and diocesan officers will find value in being more transparent about potential difficulties and in being proactive in developing supportive peer groups at the start of curacies, perhaps for TIs as well as curates, as a requirement of their supervisory role.

Training for TIs

Some of this can be addressed by seeing training for TIs as equally important as training for curates. The training I contribute to increasingly uses TI training days to talk about adopting a coaching approach and how supervision conversations can be an opportunity to explore an issue, rather than being a 'show and tell' from the curate with the TI giving instructions, corrections and advice. Training also offers an opportunity for TIs to hear from their peers about the benefits of committing to give time, genuine support and conscious development to their curate. The win-win of this approach is that, as TIs understand their own role as trainer and how this differs from simply being a good role model, they will be more willing to be trained and developed themselves. It is not unreasonable for a curate to know the bare minimum that they can expect from a TI by way of time commitment, development and relationship, and for this to feature in TI training.

An Environment for Constructive Feedback

It is often difficult for a curate to give feedback about their TI after their curacy is over. Reports are focused on how well the curate has met the training objectives and are not an opportunity to feed back on the performance of the trainer. Reflecting on his experience of a group debriefing with their DDO over lunch, Philip suggested that:

> There needs to be a one-on-one, because you can't 'dis' your colleagues in front of others, it's not right, it's not a good thing to do—so, that conversation would be helpful.

Providing Curates with the Information to Make Good Decisions

Those placing curates need to have the information and the opportunity to satisfy themselves that the placement will be appropriate, not least because it is vital to give the curate a meaningful choice about whether to accept a particular placement. It is important to note that larger scale studies have found that having had a previous curate is no indicator of the success of the next, so there should never be an assumption that a TI will automatically be given another curate or that the location of an available diocesan house denotes a training parish.[12]

Strengthening Local Support Structures

It is worth considering how to strengthen the role of those who are closer to the ground. Rural deans, for example, can offer more support but, due to the informal nature of the relationship, it can be patchy, as Beverley found in her second placement:

> Had it not been for the rural dean, I probably would have gone belly-up. He was very good, but it's on an informal basis. I think rural deans are a better bet than many. But the impression I get, maybe it's always like this, it's very personal. If they feel sympathetic towards you, you're going to get a lot of support. If they don't feel sympathetic towards you or don't understand your perspective, you're not.

There is no downside to a diocese giving attention to the specifics of how to make the training environment as supportive as possible, including at least the following:

> There is a clear need, within dioceses, to build up a more complete picture of each training relationship and to have clear lines of accountability and communication. There is no shortage of people who are working with curates, but the crux of the issue seems to be that those who are able to respond pastorally to curates lack the position in the hierarchy to do anything about it, and those who have such power are too far removed from the situation to be able to offer pastoral support. One respondent commented that the dots were not joined up.

Granted, curates are not always aware of the demanding and complex nature of setting up and overseeing healthy and constructive training partnerships. However, it is nevertheless worth recognizing that the overall message from the survey seems to be that, from their end, the placing of curates can feel like an exercise in fitting puzzle pieces into a jigsaw and trading those who do not fit with other dioceses.

Curates: Surviving and Thriving Under Pressure

4

Much has been written about how to have appropriate boundaries as a curate. Everyone needs to decide for themselves how much notice they take of received wisdom such as 'Take your day off outside the parish' or 'Don't make friends with your parishioners.' I spent my curacy a short drive from the South Devon coast, so it was no hardship to get out and about when I was not working. Conversely, as a married couple with no children at that point, we valued the opportunity to spend social time with other young families in the church and ignored the advice about keeping our distance socially.

This chapter will look specifically at some things that do lie within your power as a curate, before the next chapter develops some of these into a practical relational toolkit for curates and TIs to work through together.

Setting Your Expectations Correctly: Five Questions

One of the five potential difficulties which my research uncovered was situations where curates were repeatedly told that the problems they faced were due to their own unrealistic expectations of the role. The consistent advice seems to be that since you are only there for a few years, you should 'suck it up,' 'take the rough with the smooth' and 'make the most of the opportunity.'

Unfortunately, this short-sighted advice has long-term implications. If you are not supported during this key formational period, there is danger that you will not only learn bad habits but might also develop unhealthy coping mechanisms and experience damage to your well-being and sense of vocation. One should, however, acknowledge that there is such a thing as being 'refined by fire,' so that not every difficult curacy results in a ministry that is permanently scarred. The way to engender resilience is not to force you to endure three years of stress, but to help you build support networks and healthy working patterns that you can carry into your first incumbent-status role.

What this means in practice is keeping a healthy level of self-reflection at the heart of your spiritual life and investing in honest and supportive relationships outside your current context. This will give you places to explore any feelings of injustice or disappointment and discern what is within your power to change, what you can use to grow, and when you might need outside help to change the situation. The following paragraphs give some diagnostic questions which you can use in your own reflections or with a small trusted group.

Q1: Are My Expectations Reasonable and Realistic?

Many of the problems encountered by curates in my research arose from mismatched expectations between the curate, TI and diocese. Some of these are illustrated in chapter two. At this point it is worth making a distinction between reasonable expectations and realistic expectations. Sometimes when a TI or churchwarden says your expectations are *unreasonable*, they actually mean that they are *unrealistic* because the resources are not there to support that expectation. For example, there are lots of reasons why I would consider it very reasonable for a curate to be based in a single parish within a multi-parish team. It might, however, be unrealistic for this to happen while still maintaining the existing level of clergy cover for Sunday services across the team.

Reasonable expectations deal with fundamental questions of calling and well-being, while realistic expectations are usually in the realm of resources. In an ideal world, there would not be any difference between reasonable and realistic expectations but, in an organization with limited resources (such as the Church of England), it is important to understand the capacity of the institution you are serving as you set your expectations.

Conversation is usually the key to working out the difference between reasonable and realistic expectations. Negotiation is how you get to a place where both you and your TI (and your church treasurer) agree that something is not just reasonable, but realistic. For more on direct communication and negotiation, see chapter five.

Exercise

Think about the expectations which are currently causing you stress. Use the table below to discern which category they are in and how you might view them in the light of this.

Reasonable Expectations	Realistic Expectations

Q2: Is This an Opportunity for Personal Growth or for Loving Service?

This question is about recognizing your motivation for undertaking any particular task. Nobody has reservations about being asked to do things you enjoy with people who give life and encouragement. But when you are required to do things which are more draining, you can frame them as things which will help you develop and grow, or as things which allow you to demonstrate loving service to others. Clearly, these two are closely intertwined, but one has the sense of 'What can I get out of this?' while the other is more about 'What can I give?' It is helpful to try to maintain a healthy balance between these options, rather than always landing on the same side.

Q3: Is This Developing Resilience or Crushing My Spirit?

The difference between challenges that develop resilience and stress which crushes the life out of us is the level of support we receive from those around us. As part of the research I heard from a few former curates who were no longer exercising ordained ministry and others who seriously questioned their vocation during their curacy. One respondent was left in no doubt that this was due to difficulties caused by their TI:

> [I worked with an] excellent ministry team and lay leaders. [My] training [was] undermined by recognized incumbent dysfunction. Some rich and valued experience to take forward but could have been so much better. A great loss and completely unnecessary additional stress on myself and family during training years. It nearly broke me.

In a good curacy, you will be exposed to the most challenging situations in the parish, but will do so knowing you have prayer, encouragement and backup from your TI, as well as the opportunity to reflect, debrief and even hand over the situation if is too much for you to handle at that time. One curate expressed their gratitude to their TI, saying:

> Though we were different in many ways, we were also frank, kind and forgiving with each other. In public, and in a difficult multi-parish benefice, she had my back and I had hers. We did our disagreements in private.

In terms of finding the support you need, there are usually extensive diocesan support structures around curates, but these can vary in usefulness depending on who is facilitating them. At their best, IME2 training and peer groups can be a place to receive support that might be lacking in the parish. It is also important to commit time and energy to these groups even if you are well supported in your parish, as your colleagues may see them as more of a lifeline than you do. If the group gets the balance of challenge and support wrong, or never gets to the crux of an issue, then you may need to seek an alternative peer group outside the diocesan structure.[13]

Q4: Is This Challenging Me to Perform or Undermining My Expertise?

Following on from the question about support is a question about challenge. You will have your own reasons for finding certain situations difficult and need to discern whether this is due to the need for training, lack of inclination or whether you are being asked to do something in a way that is unnatural for the person you are. TIs who do not operate a model of adult education often fall back on the master / apprentice model where they expect their curate to mimic exactly what they do. This was expressed by one curate when she said, 'I was supposed to preach in the same manner as the incumbent which did not work for me.' This situation very often means that you are denied the opportunity to think about how you could meet needs in a way that brings your personality, gifting and passions to the task at hand. There is rarely a downside to vocalizing this gently and it may well be that your TI simply has not noticed. Even if the opportunities to correct this may be few in the daily nuts and bolts of church work, it might well be that your TI is open to trying some fresh initiative in an area of your gifting and passion. Sometimes we do not have because we do not ask!

A good curacy always involves facing new and complex situations, giving us the confidence to reimagine a creative response that draws on our own experience. This also helps us recognize where we would benefit from further training. Another curate who recognized the crucial role her TI had played in allowing her to establish her unique ministry wrote:

> My curacy was successful due in large part to the continual encouragement and guidance from my TI. There was nothing I could not discuss with him; he was consistently supportive and committed to the training relationship. I felt valued and able to ask anything. He gave me space to make mistakes—which of course sometimes I did—and he and I then discussed events and how to move forward.

Q5: Do We Have Different Personalities or an Incompatible Model of Ministry?

This question is for a little further down the track if your training relationship is feeling uncomfortable or demoralizing. Ultimately the church is a place where differences are supposed to be overcome, and differing personality types can be reconciled as you use the relational toolkit (discussed in chapter five) to understand how others in your team tick. What is more of a permanent barrier, however, is working with a trainer who has a very different model of ministry from you, or who is unwilling to accept that you will bring new ways of being and working to the churches you serve. Again, these differences can be overcome by honest conversation and corporate self-reflection, but if you find that you are hitting a brick wall, it may be time to ask for formal support from the diocese or even to ask to be moved to a new placement.

Each of these five questions for self-reflection could also be brought to a supervision session with a TI in whom you trust to respond in an undefended way. Ultimately, each question is about recognizing your own lines in the sand and a healthy establishing of where your ministerial boundaries lie, as you move through curacy and into your next role.

5 A Relational Toolkit for Curates and Training Incumbents

One contented curate responded to my research by writing, '[My TI and I] both worked hard to understand each other; that made for a positive outcome.' This chapter looks at some of the most common ways that relationships can be transformed from fractious to fantastic. What they all rely on, however, is the commitment from both parties to work on the relationship and accept that we might be the one who needs to change the most.

A Commitment to Direct Communication

Although it is sometimes well-motivated, congregations can exploit and exacerbate the differences between a curate and their TI by playing them off against each other. In her Grove booklet, *Leadership Resilience in Conflict*, Sandra Cobbin talks about healthy and unhealthy triangles.[14] 'Triangling' takes place when one person (A) talks to another (B) about a third person (C). Such a conversation becomes unhealthy when A is attempting to pass their anxiety and responsibility about C over to B. In a training relationship, this commonly occurs when parishioners moan to a curate about their TI, or when the TI says to the curate, 'People have said this about you.' It is even possible for the curate to collude in the unhealthy triangle by thinking that they are sparing their TI the stress of dealing with people's complaints. Martin articulated this when he said:

> Within a month of arriving it became fairly clear—because I was getting my ear bent quite regularly by parishioners—there were some issues, [my TI] was having some challenges. Which was quite difficult because I had just landed and I haven't passed any of that on to him because he's quite fragile and I think he's probably aware that there are some challenges, and [it] wouldn't do anybody any good.

Cobbin calls on leaders to model re-triangling, where they do not absorb the anxiety and responsibility which belongs to others. In other words, curates can break the cycle of unhealthy triangling by refusing to be the go-between for a congregation and their TI, encouraging others to own their feedback (both of TI and curate) and give it face to face.

One such opportunity for a curate to give direct feedback to their TI is supervised supervision sessions. However, although an astute facilitator can ask the difficult questions, it is often not enough for the curate simply to tell the story and hope that the other party picks up on the nuances. Sometimes there is a need to be more direct, focusing on specific actions and feelings as a precursor to discussing how both parties hope things might be different in the future. This is sometimes called the 'I saw, I felt, I need, I want' model, recognizing the power of unambiguous 'I' statements in conflict resolution. For example, Louise could have used this approach in the situation she describes here:

> I think the last time I flipped with him was because I wanted to talk about something and he was expecting me to talk in front of the cleaners hovering in and out, and so when we eventually managed to get somewhere I said to him, 'You can't do that, you can't. How can you ask me how I'm getting on when you've got [Sharon] in the background washing up.'

Using this model, Louise could have said to her TI, '*I've noticed* that you often try to have important conversations when we are short of time and when there are other people around. This makes *me feel* that I can't say what is really on my mind as we are being overheard and I don't feel we have enough time for what I want to say. What *I need* is dedicated time and space for our supervision meetings, so *I'd like* us to put regular supervision slots in the diary for the rest of this year so that we know there is a time set aside for us to talk properly.'

Even if it is not possible for the TI and curate to give each other exactly what they are asking for, it is clear what this is and why they think it is important. It also invites the listener to respond with similarly clear 'I' statements as they work towards an agreed way forward.

Supervisions

A large number of curates in my research made comments about the (lack of) time their TI gave to supervision meetings. They cited examples where meetings did not happen regularly, were frequently cancelled or postponed, or where the TI had too many other commitments inside and outside the parish to devote sufficient time to training them. TIs also seem to confuse supervision meetings with planning or with team meetings, do not allow the curate to shape the agenda, or do not use the time to reflect properly on the curate's experiences and what they can both learn from them. This reveals a lack of shared expectations about purpose, format, content and frequency of meetings.

Developing constructive supervision sessions, while critical, is beyond the scope of this booklet. Two resources that are well worth consulting are:

- 3D Coaching, an organization that works closely with many dioceses to train TIs to support and supervise curates by using a coaching model.[15] Their model of creating 'a container for a conversation' is a helpful way to describe supervision meetings. The supervision container is formed by having a pre-agreed format, an agenda, space to raise issues and concerns (on both sides), enough flexibility to respond to changing needs, and a written record of what was discussed and agreed.
- Rick Simpson's book, *Supervising a Curate: A Short Guide to a Complex Task* is helpful for detailed practical advice on supervision meetings.[16]

Recognizing the Impact of Personality Differences

Collaborative ministry cuts both ways, and there is much that both TIs and curates can do to facilitate a healthy training relationship. One of these is to recognize differences in personality, and to name these and to agree practical steps to bridge the gap. An experienced TI called Graham once told me about a curate he had trained who was temperamentally very different from him. They used to have supervision meetings on a Monday morning and Graham was self-aware enough to say, 'Just because I ask for time to go away and think about what you've said, doesn't mean that I'm stalling for time and looking for a way to say "no." I genuinely need time to reflect on this.'

Other personality differences which can lead to tension include approaches to conflict and disagreement (whether people prefer to avoid it or face it head-on), how they make decisions, how they prioritize and organize their time and how they give and receive feedback.

When exploring these differences within a team, it can be useful to use one of the self-reflection tools provided by the secular leadership world. The Myers-Briggs Type Indicator, Belbin's team roles, the Enneagram or the Four Leadership Energies are just four examples of such tools which have been used by dioceses to help teams to thrive by learning to recognize and respond to differences in personality, temperament, gifting, ways of approaching issues and responses to pressure and unforeseen circumstances.

No reflection tool is perfect and assigning personality types can be unhelpful if we use them to define and pigeonhole people. However, they can be really useful for spotting some of the ways people are different from others and for opening up conversations about how they can understand each other better.

Recognizing the Impact of Theological and Stylistic Differences

Very few people come through the discernment process and initial training with exactly the same theological outlook as they started, and ordination is not a process of fixing what they will think and believe for the rest of their ministry. In a perfect placement, both a curate and their TI might expect their interactions with each other to lead to a growing understanding of another point of view and reflection on how their own mission and ministry might be enhanced by insights from other church traditions. In practice, however, the church tradition of the TI—especially if this is shared by the church congregation—is likely to be the normal practice with which the curate is expected to conform. When the outworking of this is questioned it can be interpreted as undermining the theological convictions of the TI or church.

A tool which can help to move discussions about 'how we do things around here' away from the threatening territory of tradition is the 'four voices of theology.' Helen Cameron and others identified different sources of theological knowledge within a church community as 'the four voices' and stated that they all need to be attended to by anyone undertaking thoughtful Theological Action Research (TAR).[17] The four voices are:

- *Espoused theology*—the theology embedded within a group's articulation of its beliefs.
- *Operant Theology*—the theology embedded in the actual practices of the group.
- *Normative Theology*—scriptural, canonical or liturgical texts which are named by the group as its theological authority and which can inform and correct operant and espoused theologies.
- *Formal Theology*—academic theological resources used to explain or expound their belief.

It does not take much imagination to think of examples where a church's operant and espoused theologies are out of alignment, or where normative theology is not really transforming the practices of a group.

For example, one curate talked about the differences between their TI's espoused theology of eucharistic presidency and the operant theology seen in his practice. When talking about their curate, the TI was quick to stress the importance of being trained for every aspect of ministry—their espoused theology was one where priestly ministry was shared among those who were ordained. In practice, however, the curate reported that their TI hardly ever let her preside at the eucharist and the focus of the procession was always the TI.

When exploring why something is the way it is, it can be helpful to see that practice, articulation and belief are all carriers of theology. When there is a consistency between the different voices, it is clear why a particular practice is right or appropriate. When you recognize a dissonance, it can be an opportunity to think creatively about how changes to your practice are needed to align operant theology with espoused theology.

The Value of Different Types of Accountability in Different Types of Curacy

Times are a-changing for curates and curacies. I am aware of curates who are successfully dividing their time between a parish church and a bishop's mission order (BMO), one who is leading a church plant in their deacon year, and others who are joining formational communities, being licensed across a whole deanery and who will be part of a diocese's response to the 2020 coronavirus pandemic in establishing online churches.[18]

Here the same common difficulties are still a danger, but some are amplified. The most pressing problem for curates in these new contexts is confused lines of accountability.

Curates in a normal parish placement can be overwhelmed by the sheer number of different people who are involved in their training, especially when it comes to knowing who they can raise issues with and who has the authority to do anything about them. Where a curate has a split placement or is working across an even wider area, these relationships need careful negotiation, especially when deciding how a curate's time will be allocated, who will meet them for supervision and who will offer feedback on their ministry.

The opposite problem can also exist for those who are accountable to a board of trustees (in the case of a BMO) or directly to a bishop or archdeacon. Here, it is possible for everyone to assume the curate is being looked after by someone else, but the hands-off nature of the relationship means that their training incumbent is now not close enough to model ministry, offer feedback and give real support.

None of this is to say that innovative curacies should be stifled; quite the opposite. If curates in these roles are to thrive, however, extra attention needs to be given to creating role descriptions and agreeing expectations around supervisions, observations and learning outcomes.

6

Afterword

Hopefully you will be able to practise some of the tools before you get to the point where you need to call upon them to resolve conflict. Whatever caused you to pick up this booklet, my prayer for you is that God would continue to grow in us the gifts of empathy, encouragement and empowerment so that we can bear with each other and build each other up as ministers in his church.

A Benediction for Those Seeking to Follow the Pattern of Christ in Their Leadership

May the Lord who chose us to be born of water and the spirit,
Teach us to value ourselves rightly
And see his image in those we serve alongside.
May the Lord who called us by name into his service,
Help us to discern his voice
As he calls us afresh to grow his kingdom.
May the Lord who equipped us for works of service,
Teach us to rely on his strength
And daily ask for his grace.
May the Lord who gave us one to the other,
Strengthen the bond of love between us
As we serve shoulder to shoulder.
And may the blessing of God Almighty
Who is Father, Son and Holy Spirit,
Be with us all, evermore. Amen.

Notes

1 Ordained minsters in the Church of England are required to undertake Initial Ministerial Education (IME) before they are licensed. This training (IME Phase 1) begins in a Theological Education Institution (TEI) and is followed by a curacy (IME Phase 2), where the newly-ordained minister is licensed to a parish or team ministry and assigned a training incumbent (TI).

2 As the scope of the research prevented undertaking a large-scale survey which would be generalizable across the whole Church of England, four dioceses were chosen to provide illustrative data. These were all in the Southern Province but outside London. Participants were at least 18 months into their curacy and some had moved on to their next post. Data from 56 curates was collected and eight

individuals took part in follow-up interviews. Five interviewees were women and three were men. All interviewees were full-time curates, one of whom was financially self-supporting. Between them, interviewees had experience of both male and female TIs.

3 G Smith, 'Exploring Training Relationships Between Training Incumbents and Curates in the Church of England and the Church in Wales: Listening to Training Incumbents in the Post Hind Era' (Thesis submitted for the degree of PhD, University of Warwick, 2015) p 249; R Perrin, 'Vocational Pathways: Perspectives from Curacy' (2016), https://www.churchofengland.org/sites/default/files/2017-10/perspectives_from_curacy.pdf (accessed 3 December 2020) p 27.

4 All quotations from curates are from participants in my own research and all names have been changed.

5 M Caminer, M Percy and B Stevenson, *Curacies and How to Survive Them* (London: SPCK, 2015) p 77.

6 Smith, *op cit*, p 246.

7 S P Walker, *The Undefended Leader* (Carlisle: Piquant Editions, 2010).

8 C Bennetts, K Elliston, and M Maconachie, 'Continuing professional development for public health: An andragogical approach' in *Public Health,* 126 (2012) p 541.

9 K Lamdin and D Tilley, *Supporting New Ministers in the Local Church: A Handbook* (London: SPCK, 2007) p 144.

10 A Fernando, *Jesus Driven Ministry* (Leicester: Inter-Varsity Press, 2002) pp 131–152.

11 A good place to start when matching training needs with what a placement can offer are the 'Formation Criteria for Ordained Ministry in the Church of England.' These describe what is expected of curates by the end of IME Phase 2 and should map onto the reports written by TEIs in Phase 1. Before being offered a curate a training parish could be asked to list, in detail, how it would seek to provide training under each of the criteria, and how they will measure and assess these aims. This could take the place of the more usual descriptive profile and, I would suggest, could be more useful in the matching of people to posts.

12 Smith, *op cit*, p 318. Smith suggests that while there can be a healthy continuity in 'training parishes' they can become 'toxically unhealthy' unless 'the evaluation of a placement is adequately robust on every occasion,' *ibid*, p 138.

13 Living Leadership (livingleadership.org, accessed 3 December 2020) offer a number of routes to supportive relationships, including groups, conferences and one-to-one mentoring.

14 S Cobbin, *Leadership Resilience in Conflict* (Grove Leadership booklet L22).

15 See www.3Dcoaching.com (accessed 3 December 2020) for more resources.

16 R Simpson, *Supervising a Curate: A Short Guide to a Complex Task* (Grove Pastoral booklet P128).

17 H Cameron and others, *Talking About God in Practice: Theological Action Research and Practical Theology* (London: SCM Press, 2010) p 54.

18 A different form of Anglican church, outside the normal parish set-up.